365 Days of Sports: Motivational Quotes For the Sports Lover

Foreword by M.G. Keefe

365 Days of Sports:

Motivational Quotes for the Sports Lover

Hot Tropica Books Publication

February 2013

Copyright © 2013 Foreword by M.G. Keefe

Cover illustration copyright © Jackson Falls

ISBN 10: 1482581868
ISBN 13: 978-1482581867

Published by: **Hot Tropica Books**

365 Days of Sports

Blurb:

This collection of sports quotes is meant to inspire and motivate the sports lovers in all of us. Start the day off with a smile by reading a sports quote a day every day of the year or just in one sitting.

The quotes are from celebrities, comedians, athletes, coaches, politicians, and just about anybody who has an opinion on sports.

This book also makes a terrific gift for young athletes and men and women of all ages.

Sports do not build character. They reveal it. ~ John Wooden

Foreword by MG Keefe

Sports have long been part of civilized society. It strengthens our bodies and our minds. We learn to work together and as individuals to push our performance levels to the next level.

Our bodies need exercise to maintain itself physically. There is much that we get out of playing sports. It builds character, self esteem, self-worth and is good for our children.

But anybody who plays sports regularly understands sports is much more than exercise. People who play competitive sports regularly are much more likely to strengthen themselves mentally as well. If push comes to shove, these are the people who are more likely to fight back and stand up for themselves.

The Olympic games started in 776 BC. It may have started as a way to honor the Greek Gods and the dead, but it quickly grew into something much larger than that. It stopped when the Romans got involved and then it was revived in the early nineteenth century and has been around ever since. It has become a competition of every country's best athletes to find the very best in the world.

But even if you aren't a competitor, sports of any kind is entertaining to watch. The viewer is just as involved in the heartbreak and the elation that comes with losing or winning. Sports is ingrained in our society and a really big part of our world. I can't imagine a world without it.

Sports do not build character. They reveal it. ~ John Wooden

365 Days of Sports

January 1: Success isn't something that just happens. Success is learned, success is practiced, and then it is shared. ~ Sparky Anderson

January 2: Nobody who ever gave his best regretted it. ~ George Halas

January 3: Never give up, never give in, and when the upper hand is ours, may we have the ability to handle the win with the dignity that we absorbed the loss. ~ Doug Williams

January 4: Leadership, like coaching is fighting for the hearts and souls of men and getting them to believe in you. ~ Eddie Robinson

January 5: Always make a total effort, even when the odds are against you. ~ Arnold Palmer

January 6: You can motivate by fear, and you can motivate by reward. But both of those methods are only temporary. The only lasting thing is self motivation. ~ Homer Rice

January 7: Without self-discipline, success is impossible, period. ~ Lou Holtz

January 8: Do you know what my favorite part of the gam is? The opportunity to play. ~ Mike Singletary

January 9: During my 18 years I came to bat almost 10,000 times. I struck out maybe 1700 times, walked maybe 1800 times. You figure a ballplayer will average about 500 at bats a season. That means I played seven years without ever hitting the ball. ~ Mickey Mantle

January 10: One man can be a crucial ingredient on a team, but one man cannot make a team. ~ Kareem Abdul-Jabbar

January 11: The more difficult the victory, the greater the happiness in winning. ~ Pele

January 12: A trophy carries dust. Memories last forever. ~ Mary Lou Retton

January 13: What makes something special is not just what you have to gain, but what you feel there is to lose. ~ Andre Agassi

January 14: If you fail to prepare, you're prepared to fail. ~ Mark Spitz

January 15: Champions keep playing until they get it right. ~ Billy Jean King

January 16: Make sure your worst enemy doesn't live between your own two ears. ~ Laird Hamilton

January 17: The difference between the impossible and possible lies in a person's determination. ~ Tommy Lasorda

January 18: It's not the will to win that matters—everyone has that. It's the will to prepare that matters. ~ Paul "Bear" Bryant

January 19: Set your goals high, and don't stop till you get there. ~ Bo Jackson

January 20: Age is no barrier. It's a limitation you put on your mind. ~ Jackie-Joynee Kersee

January 21: An athlete cannot run with money in his pockets. He must run with hope in his heart and dreams in his head. ~ Emil Zatopek

January 22: Football doesn't build character, it reveals it. ~ Marv Levy

January 23: Persistence can change failure into extraordinary achievement. ~ Matt Biondi

January 24: Pain is temporary. It may last a minute, or an hour, or a day, or a year, but eventually it will subside and something else will take its place. If I quit, however, it lasts forever. ~ Lance Armstrong

January 25: One man practicing sportsmanship is better than fifty preaching it. ~ Knute Rockne

January 26: Concentration is the ability to think about absolutely nothing when it is absolutely necessary. ~ Ray Knight

January 27: It's not so important who starts a game but who finishes it. ~ John Wooden

January 28: You are never really playing an opponent. You are playing yourself, your own high standards, and when you reach your limits, that is real joy. ~ Arthur Ashe

January 29: Nobody's natural. You work hard to get good and then work hard to get better. It's hard to stay on top. ~ Paul Coffey

January 30: Losers quit when they're tired. Winners quit when they've won. ~ Unknown

January 31: The greatest efforts in sports came when the mind is as still as a glass lake. ~ Timothy Gallwey

February 1: You find that you have peace of mind and can enjoy yourself, get more sleep, and rest when you know it was a one hundred percent effort that you gave—win or lose ~ Gordie Howe

February 2: Show me a guy who's afraid to look bad, and I'll show you a guy you can beat every time. ~ Lou Brock

February 3: If you have everything under control, you're not moving fast enough. ~ Mario Andretti

February 4: Just keep going. Everyone gets better if they keep at it. ~ Ted Williams

February 5: To uncover your true potential you must first find your own limits and then you have to have the courage to blow past them. ~ Picabo Street

February 6: If you can believe it, the mind can achieve it. ~ Ronnie Lott

February 7: Push yourself again and again. Don't give an inch until the final buzzer sounds. ~ Larry Bird

February 8: What to do with a mistake: recognize it, admit it, learn from it, forget it. ~ Dean Smith

February 9: I hated every minute of training, but I said, "Don't quit. Suffer now and live the rest of your life as a champion." ~ Muhammed Ali

February 10: If you aren't going all the way, why go at all? ~ Joe Namath

February 11: I've learned that something constructive comes from every defeat. ~ Tom Landry

February 12: It's not the size of a man, but the size of his heart that matters. ~ Evander Holyfield

February 13: The will to win is important, but the will to prepare is vital. ~ Joe Paterno

February 14: Your biggest opponent isn't the other guy. It's human nature. ~ Bobby Knight

February 15: Never let the fear of striking out get in your way. ~ Babe Ruth

February 16: There are only two options regarding commitment. You're either IN or you're OUT. There is no such thing as life in-between. ~ Pat Riley

February 17: Never let your head hang down. Never sit down and grieve. Find another way. ~ Satchel Paige

February 18: Do not let what you cannot do interfere with what you can do. ~ John Wooden

February 19: A champion is someone who gets up when he can't. ~ Jack Dempsey

February 20: It ain't over till it's over. ~ Yogi Berra

February 21: I've missed over 5000 shots in my career. I've lost almost 300 games. 26 times, I've been trusted to take the game winning shot and missed. I've failed over and over again in my life. And that is why I succeed. ~ Michael Jordan

February 22: You're never a loser until you quit trying. ~ Mike Ditka

February 23: It's not whether you get knocked down; it's whether you get up. ~ Vince Lombardi

February 24: You miss 100 percent of the shots you don't take. ~ Wayne Gretzky

February 25: Never give up! Failure and rejection are only the first step to succeeding. ~ Jim Valvano

February 26: Good guys are a dime a dozen, but an aggressive leader is priceless. ~ Red Blaik

February 27: The strength of the group is the strength of the leaders. ~ Vince Lombardi

February 28: Make the present good, and the past will take care of itself. ~ Knute Rockne

March 1: Basically I have two speeds…Hostile or smart-aleck. Your choice. ~ James Patterson

March 2: The harder you work. The harder it is to surrender. ~ Vince Lombardi

March 3: If you are going to be champion, you must be willing to pay a greater price. ~ Bud Wilkinson

March 4: Everytime you stay out late; everytime you sleep in; everytime you miss a workout; everytime you don't give 100%...you make it that much easier for me to beat you. ~ Unknown

March 5: Success is about having, excellence is about being. Success is about having money and fame, but excellence is about being the best you can be. ~ Mike Ditka

March 6: You can't make a great play unless you do it first in practice. ~ Chuck Noll

March 7: Never let your head hang down. Never give up and sit down and grieve. Find another way. ~ Satchel Paige

March 8: Things that hurt, instruct. ~ Benjamin Franklin

March 9: Everybody pulls for David. Nobody roots for Goliath. ~ Wilt Chamberlain

March 10: When I was young, I never wanted to leave the court until I got things exactly correct. My dream was to become pro. ~ Larry Bird

March 11: My responsibility is getting all my players playing for the name on the front of the jersey, not the one on the back. ~ Unknown

March 12: Good, better, best. Never let it rest. Until your good is better ad your better is best. ~ Tim Duncan

March 13: The pitcher has got only a ball. I've got a bat. So the percentage of weapons is in my favor and I let the fellow with the ball do the fretting. ~ Hank Aaron

March 14: You owe it to yourself to be the best you possibly can be in baseball and in life. ~ Pete Rose

March 15: It takes a lot of hard work and dedication just like any pro sport. Especially for beach volleyball you don't have to be as tall or fast as other sports. You just have to have the skills. ~ Misty May

March 16: Make sure team members know they are working with you, not for you. ~ John Wooden

March 17: What makes a good coach? Complete dedication. ~ George Halas

March 18: I learn teaching from teachers. I learn golf from golfers. I learn winning from coaches. ~ Harvey Penick

March 19: My responsibility is leadership, and the minute I get negative, that is going to have an influence on my team. ~ Don Shula

March 20: In the end, the game comes down to one thing: man against man. May the best man win. ~ Sam Huff

March 21: Victory belongs to the most persevering. ~ Napolean

March 22: A life of frustration is inevitable for any coach whose main enjoyment is winning. ~ Chuck Noll

March 23: Every game is an opportunity to measure yourself against your own potential. ~ Bud Wilkinson

March 24: It is how you show up at the showdown that counts. ~ Homer Norton

March 25: Without self-discipline, success is impossible, period. ~ Lou Holtz

March 26: If you aren't going all the way, why go at all? ~ Joe Namath

March 27: If you don't practice you don't deserve to win. ~ Andre Agassi

March 28: You can always become better. ~ Tiger Woods

March 29: If you ask me anything I don't know, I'm not going to answer. ~ Yogi Berra

March 30: I've always believed that if you put in the work, the results will come. ~ Michael Jordan

March 31: If you don't invest very much, then defeat doesn't hurt very much and winning is not very excited. ~ Dick Vermeil

April 1: The spirit, the will to win, and the will to excel are things that endure. These qualities are so much more important than the events that occur. ~ Vince Lombardi

April 2: The difference between a successful person and others is not a lack of strength, not a lack of knowledge, but rather a lack of will. ~ Vince Lombardi

April 3: The man who has no imagination has no wings. ~ Muhammad Ali

April 4: I always turn to the sports section first. The sports section records people's accomplishments; the front page has nothing but man's failures. ~ Earl Warren

April 5: The difference between the old ballplayer and the new ballplayer is the jersey. The old ballplayer cared about the name on the front. The new ballplayer cares about the name on the back. ~ Steve Garvey

April 6: If a tie is like kissing your sister, losing is like kissing your grandmother with her teeth out. ~ George Brett

April 7: The fewer rules a coach has, the fewer rules there are for players to break. ~ John Madden

April 8: We didn't lose the game. We just ran out of time. ~ Vince Lombardi

April 9: When we played World Series checks meant something. Now all they do is screw up your taxes. ~ Don Drysdale

April 10: The more you sweat in practice, the less you bleed in battle. ~ Unknown

April 11: I wanted to have a career in sports when I was young, but I had to give it up. I'm only six feet tall, so I couldn't play basketball. I'm only 190 pounds, so I couldn't play football. And I have 20/20 vision, so I couldn't be a referee. ~ Jay Leno

April 12: Playing Polo is like trying to play golf during an earthquake. ~ Sylvester Stallone

April 13: The breakfast of champions is not cereal, it's the opposition. ~ Nick Seitz

April 14: I figure practice puts your brains in your muscles. ~ Sam Snead

April 15: In play there are two pleasures for your choosing. One is winning, and the other is losing. ~ Lord Byron

April 16: All sports are games of inches. ~ Dick Ritger

April 17: Most people give up just when they're about to achieve success. They quit on the one yard line. They give up at the last minute of the game, one foot from winning a touchdown. ~ Ross Perot

April 18: Pain is nothing compared what it feels like to quit. ~ Unknown

April 19: Don't look back. Something may be gaining on you. ~ Satchel Paige

April 20: When the going gets weird, the weird turn pro. ~ Hunter S Thompson

April 21: A good hockey player plays where the puck is. A great hockey player plays where the puck is going to be. ~ Wayne Gretzky

April 22: You can't put a limit on anything. The more you dream, the further you get. ~ Michael Phelps

April 23: It's just a job. Grass grows, birds fly, waves pound the sand. I beat people up. ~ Muhammad Ali

April 24: I want to rip out his heart and feed it to Lennox Lewis. I want to kill people. I want to rip their stomachs out and eat their children. ~ Mike Tyson

April 25: Just play. Have fun. Enjoy the game. ~ Michael Jordan

April 26: People ask me what I do in winter when there's no baseball. I'll tell you what I do. I stare out the window and wait for spring. ~ Rogers Hornsby

April 27: Gold medals aren't really made of gold. They're made of sweat, determination, and a hard-to-find alloy called guts. ~ Dan Gable

April 28: If winning isn't everything, why do they keep score? ~ Vince Lombardi

April 29: Hockey is a sport for white men. Basketball is a sport for black men. Golf is a sport for white men dressed as black pimps. ~ Tiger Woods

April 30: As athletes we are used to reacting quickly. Here, it's come, stop, come, stop. There's a lot of downtime. That's the hardest part of the day. ~ Michael Jordan

May 1: Show me a good loser, and I'll show you a good loser. ~ Vince Lombardi

May 2: Serious sport has nothing to do with fair play. It is bound up with hatred, jealousy, boastfulness, disregard of all rules and sadistic pleasure in witnessing violence. In other words, it is war, minus the shooting. ~ George Orwell

May 3: My motto was always to keep swinging. Whether I was in a slump or feeling badly or having trouble off the field, the only thing to do was to keep swinging. ~ Hank Aaron

May 4: Golf is a good walk spoiled. ~ Mark Twain

May 5: Many men go fishing all their lives without realizing it is not fish they are after. ~ Henry David Thoreau

May 6: Adversity causes some men to break; others to break records. ~ William Arthur Ward

May 7: Half the lies they tell about me aren't true. ~ Yogi Berra

May 8: I'm tired of hearing about money, money, money, money, money. I just want to play the game, drink Pepsi, wear Reebok. ~ Shaquille O'Neal

May 9: It's good sportsmanship not to pick up lost golf balls while they are still rolling. ~ Mark Twain

May 10: Thus so wretched is man that he would weary without any cause for weariness…and so frivolous is he that, though full of a thousand reasons for weariness, the least thing such as playing billiards or hitting a ball is sufficient enough to amuse him. ~ Blaise Pascal

May 11: I went to a fight the other night, and a hockey game broke out. ~ Rodney Dangerfield

May 12: After all, is football a game or religion? ~ Howard Cosell

May 13: You always say, "I'll quit when I start to slide," and then one morning you wake up and realize you've done slid. ~ Sugar Ray Robinson

May 14: Self-praise is for losers. Be a winner. Stand for something. Always have class, and be humble. ~ John Madden

May 15: The way a team plays as a whole determines its success. You may have the greatest bunch of individual stars in the world, but if they don't play together, the club won't be worth a dime. ~ Babe Ruth

May 16: I'm not a role model...Just because I dunk a basketball doesn't mean I should raise your kids. ~ Charles Barkley

May 17: There are three types of baseball players: Those who make it happen, those who watch it happen, and those who wonder what happens. ~ Tommy Lasorda

May 18: Are you crying? Are you crying! There's no crying in baseball! No crying! ~ Tom Hanks, A League of Their Own

May 19: I don't promote boxing, I promote people. Boxing is just a catalyst to bring people together. ~ Don King

May 20: In the sports arena, I would say there is nothing like training and preparation. You have to train your mind as much as your body. ~ Venus Williams

May 21: American's addiction to sports, with the NFL at the top, is based on the excitement generated by the potential for the unexpected great play which can only happen with honest competition from great athletes. ~ Arlen Specter

May 22: What's right isn't always popular. What's popular isn't always right. ~ Howard Cosell

May 23: I ain't never liked violence. ~ Sugar Ray Robinson

May 24: Don't worry about the horse being blind, just load the wagon. ~ John Madden

May 25: Baseball was, is and always will be to me the greatest game in the world. ~ Babe Ruth

May 26: These are my new shoes. They're good shoes. They won't make you rich like me, they won't make you rebound like me, they definitely won't make you handsome like me. They'll only make you have shoes like me. That's it. ~ Charles Barkley

May 27: Guys ask me, don't I get burned out? How can you get burned out doing something you love? I ask you, have you ever got tired of kissing a pretty girl? ~ Tommy Lasorda

May 28: When did I know I had talent? I think it started when I first started playing sports, organized sports. ~ LeBron James

May 29: There are two things that come very easily to me: rooting for New York sports teams and making mistakes. ~ Harvey Weinstein

May 30: I will fight for America until the day I drop. ~ Don King

June 1: Reading isn't good for a ballplayer. Not good for his eyes. If my eyes went bad even a little bit I couldn't' hit home runs. So I gave up reading. ~ Babe Ruth

June 2: Then there is still a higher type of courage—the courage to brave pain, to live with it, to never let others know of it and to still find joy in life; to wake up in the morning with an enthusiasm for the day ahead. ~ Howard Cosell

June 3: My business is hurting people. ~ Sugar Ray Robinson

June 4: That's the biggest gap in sports, the difference between the winner and the loser in the Super Bowl. ~ John Madden

June 5: Poor people cannot rely on the government to help you in times of need. You have to get your education. Then nobody can control your destiny. ~ Charles Barkley

June 6: I love doubleheaders. That way I get to keep on my uniform longer. ~ Tommy Lasorda

June 7: It ain't about if he knocks a guy out. It's about how he knocks a guy out. It's the style, the improvisation. ~ Don King

June 8: I'm the kind of guy that if I don't work out, I will get bigger and look like one of those guys who used to play sports. ~ Seann William Scott

June 9: Unfortunately the world is what it is now. People don't get along for whatever reasons. As professional athletes, in a way we're almost ambassadors for peace, because sports brings everyone together. ~ Venus Williams

June 10: I was a total athlete. I loved sports, but when I realized I wasn't going to be a professional athlete I realized I wanted to be in the movies. ~ Seann William Scott

June 11: I was right to back Muhammad Ali, but it caused me major enmity in this nation. ~ Howard Cosell

June 12: To be champ you have to believe in yourself when no one else will. ~ Sugar Ray Robinson

June 13: Coaches have to watch what they don't want to see and listen to what they don't want to hear. ~ John Madden

June 14: Yesterday's home runs don't win today's games. ~ Babe Ruth

June 15: I don't care what people think. People are stupid. ~ Charles Barkley

June 16: About the only problem with success is that it does not teach you how to deal with failure. ~ Tommy Lasorda

June 17: You can be the greatest guy in the world, but if you ain't got no heart, you ain't gonna survive. ~ Don King

June 18: I'm girlie in the sense that I like makeup, but I also love sports and man-food. ~ Carrie Underwood

June 19: There's not a long track record of people leaving professional sports to become a software developer. ~ Curt Schilling

June 20: I play sports. ~ Josh Hutherson

June 21: My parents couldn't handle my energy so they enrolled me in every sport the school was offering. I didn't resent it because I loved sports and I picked them up easily. ~ Channing Tatum

June 22: Mommy, why does daddy cuss the TV and call it Howard? ~ Howard Cosell

June 23: If you see a defense team with dirt and mud on their backs then they've had a bad day. ~ John Madden

June 24: You just can't beat the person who never gives up. ~ Babe Ruth

June 25: My initial response was to sue her for defamation of character, but then I realized I had no character. ~ Charles Barkley

June 26: No, we don't cheat. And, even if we did, I'd never tell you. ~ Tommy Lasorda

June 27: You go for the quality of the performance, not the longevity of it. ~ Don King

June 28: I love sports. I love animals. I love kids. I want to save the world. So how do I combine all those things? I don't know. ~ Joan Jett

June 29: You cannot mix sports with politics. ~ Jackie Chan

June 30: If you're a sports fan you realize that when you meet somebody, like a girlfriend, they kind of have to root for your team. They don't have a choice. ~ Jimmy Fallon

July 1: If a guy doesn't work hard and play well, he can't lead anything. All he is, is a talker. ~ John Madden

July 2: The ultimate victory in competition is derived from the inner satisfaction of knowing that you have done your best and that you have gotten the most out of what you had to give.~ Howard Cosell

July 3: Every strike brings me closer to the next home run. ~ Babe Ruth

July 4: Sometimes that light at the end of the tunnel is a train. ~ Charles Barkley

July 5: Listen, of you start worrying about the people in the stands, before too long you're up in the stands with them. ~ Tommy Lasorda

July 6: The only yardstick for success our society has is being a champion. No one remembers anything else. ~ John Madden

July 7: I always tell people that our sports aren't that dangerous. ~ Shaun White

July 8: I don't know anything that builds the will better than competitive sports. ~ Richard M. Nixon

July 9: The best kids are going to be the best. But the best thing about it is you're going to learn lessons in playing those sports about winning and losing and teamwork and teammates and arguments and everything else that are going to affect you positively for the rest of your life. ~ Carl Lewis

July 10: But sports carried me away from being in a gang, or being associated with drugs. Sports was my way out. ~ LeBron James

July 11: Growing up, if I hadn't had sports, I don't know where I'd be. God only knows what street corners I'd be standing on, and God only knows what I'd have been doing, but instead I played hockey and went to school and stayed out of trouble. ~ Bobby Orr

July 12: Sports in human life is microcosm. ~ Howard Cosell

July 13: The road to easy street goes through the sewer. ~ John Madden

July 14: As soon as I got out there I felt a strange relationship with the pitcher's mound. It was as if I had been born out there. Pitching just felt like the most natural thing in the world. Striking out batters was easy. ~ Babe Ruth

July 15: If somebody hits you with an object you should beat the hell out of them. ~ Charles Barkley

July 16: Pressure is a word that is misused in our vocabulary. When you start thinking of pressure, it's because you started to think of failure. ~ Tommy Lasorda

July 17: I've always been a guy who wants to play sports, not watch them. ~ Shaun White

July 18: When your arm gets hit, the ball isn't going to go where you want it to. ~John Madden

July 19: Breaking records is not something you expect to be doing. That's like a sports thing, it's not usually a comedy and writing thing. ~ Louis C.K.

July 20: I'm a mad lover of sport. You cannot say a bad word to me about sports. So I know business is involved, and I know it can be cynical, and, of course, I watch it, but for me it's pure. ~ Hugh Jackman

July 21: Never force your kids into sports. I never was. To this day, my dad has never asked me to play golf. I ask him. It's the child's desire to play that matters, not the parent's desire to have the child play. Fun. Keep it fun. ~ Tiger Woods

July 22: Sports is the toy department of human life. ~ Howard Cosell

July 23: Every time I go to the theatre, there's something about the atmosphere, seeing something unfold live in front of an audience that you can't get out of your system. ~ John Madden

July 24: Let me show you how it's done…Loser! ~ Babe Ruth

July 25: I don't think of myself as giving interviews. I just have conversations. That gets me in trouble. ~ Charles Barkley

July 26: Always give an autograph when somebody asks you. ~ Tommy Lasorda

July 27: I used to play sports then I realized you can buy trophies. Now I'm good at everything. ~ Demetri Martin

July 28: The problem with winter sports is—follow me closely here—they take place in winter. ~ Dave Barry

July 29: The difference in golf and the government is that in golf you can't improve your lie. ~ George Deukmejian

July 30: Trying to sneak a fastball past Hank Aaron is like trying to sneak the sunrise past a rooster. ~ Joe Adcock

August 1: If you're going to throw a club, it's important to throw it ahead of you, down the fairway, so you don't have to waste energy going back to pick it up. ~ Tommy Bolt

August 2: Ladies and Gentlemen, the Bronx is burning. ~ Howard Cosell

August 3: I think comparisons are odious. ~ John Madden

August 4: All ballplayers should quit when it starts to feel as if all the baselines run uphill. ~ Babe Ruth

August 5: We're not all supposed to think alike. ~ Charles Barkley

August 6: When we win, I'm so happy, I eat a lot. When we lose, I'm so depressed, I eat a lot. When we're rained out, I'm so disappointed, I eat a lot. ~ Tommy Lasorda

August 7: I'd like to work with kids in special education— younger kids. ~ John Madden

August 8: He's got everything. He's not a great player yet because he hasn't won any major championships, but it's a matter of time. He's an outstanding talent. I didn't realize how tall he is. ~ Nick Price

August 9: Overall the fundamentals seem to be there and he's obviously got a mature head on his shoulders. He's got a kind of presence. ~ Nick Price

August 10: What's unfortunate about buying a pitcher for $12 million is that he carries no warranty. ~ Bob Verdi

August 11: Play is the only way the highest intelligence of humankind can unfold. ~ Joseph Chilton Pearce

August 12: The importance that society attaches to sport is incredible. After all, is football a game or religion? The people of this country have allowed sports to get completely out of hand. ~ Howard Cosell

August 13: I'm sure that had I not been a coach, I would have been some form of a teacher. ~ John Madden

August 14: Baseball changes through the years. It gets milder. ~ Babe Ruth

August 15: I don't know what that gas is made of, but it can't smell any worse than Ernie Johnson's gym bag. ~ Charles Barkley

August 16: Baseball is like driving. It's the one who gets home safely that counts. ~ Tommy Lasorda

August 17: The bell that tolls for all in boxing belongs to a cash register. ~ Bob Verdi

August 18: He hits the ball a long way and he knows how to win. ~ Gary McCord

August 19: I was showing early symptoms of becoming a professional baseball man. I was lying to the press. ~ Roger Karhn

August 20: Tennis and golf are best played, not watched. ~ Roger Kahn

August 21: He hits it long. His shoulders are impressively quick through the ball. That's where he's getting his power from. He's young and he has great elasticity. ~ Nick Faldo

August 22: Many baseball fans look upon the umpire as a necessary evil to the luxury of baseball, like the odor that follows an automobile. ~ Christy Mathewson

August 23: If you think about it, I've never held a job in my life. I've went from being a NFL player, to a coach, to a broadcaster. I haven't worked a day in my life. ~ John Madden

August 24: I had only one superstition. I made sure to touch all the bases when I hit a home run. ~ Babe Ruth

August 25: I know I'm never as good or as bad as one single performance. I've never believed in my critics or my worshippers, and I've always been able to leave my ame at the arena. ~ Charles Barkley

August 26: I believe managing is like holding a dove in your hand. Squeeze too hard and you kill it, not hard enough and it flies away. ~ Tommy Lasorda

August 27: Football is violence and cold weather and sex and college rye. ~ Roger Kahn

August 28: Baseball is a public trust. Players turn over, owners turn over, and certain commissioners turn over. But baseball goes on. ~ Peter Ueberroth

August 29: Other sports play once a week, but this sport is with us every day. ~ Peter Ueberroth

August 30: I went through baseball as a "player to be named later." ~ Joe Garagiola

August 31: Olympism is the marriage of sport and culture. ~ Juan Antonio Samaranch

September 1: You know they aren't going to lose 162 consecutive games. ~ Harry Caray

September 2: One thing you learned being a Cubs fan: when you bought a ticket, you could bank on seeing the bottom of the ninth. ~ Joe Garagiola

September 3: I'm not buddy-buddy with the players. If they need a buddy, let them buy a dog. ~ Whitey Herzog

September 4: Don't forget two things I am going to tell you. One, don't believe everything that is written about you. Two, don't pick up too many checks. ~ Babe Ruth

September 5: I think you have an obligation to be honest. ~ Charles Barkley

September 6: My theory of hitting, was just to watch the ball as it came in and hit it. ~ Tommy Lasorda

September 7: The two most important things in life are good friends, and a strong bullpen. ~ Bob Lemon

September 8: Don't play too much golf. Two rounds a day are plenty. ~ Harry Vardon

September 9: Golf is played by twenty million American men whose wives think they are out having fun. ~ Jim Bishop

September 10: You don't suffer, kill yourself, and take the risks I take just for the money. I love bike racing. ~ Greg LeMond

September 11: Perhaps the single most important element in mastering the techniques and tactics of racing is experience. But once you have the fundamentals, acquiring the experience is a matter of time. ~ Greg LeMond

September 12: New Yorkers love it when you spill your guts out there. Spill your guts at Wimbledon and they make you stop and clean it up. ~ Jimmy Connors

September 13: It is almost impossible to remember how tragic place the world is, when one is playing golf. ~ Robert Wilson Lynd

September 14: Who is richer, the man who is seen, but cannot see? Or the man who is not being seen, but can see? ~ Babe Ruth

September 15: I'm a mad dog whose only concern is winning. ~ Charles Barkley

September 16: People say you can't go out and eat with our players. I say why not? ~ Tommy Lasorda

September 17: The triple is the most exciting run in baseball. Home runs win a lot of games, but I never understood why fans are so obsessed with them. ~ Hank Aaron

September 18: You always get a special kick on opening day, no matter how many you go through. You look forward to it like a birthday party when you're a kid. You think something wonderful is going to happen. ~ Joe DiMaggio

September 19: Hitting is timing, pitching is upsetting timing. ~ Warren Spahn

September 20: Anytime Detroit scores more than 100 points and holds the other team below 100 points, they almost always win. ~ Doug Collins

September 21: Pro football is like nuclear warfare. There are no winners, only survivors. ~ Frank Gifford

September 22: I don't want to play golf. When I hit a ball, I want somebody else to go chase it. ~ Rogers Hornsby

September 23: Eighteen holes of match play will teach you more about your foe than 18 years of dealing with him across a desk. ~ Grantland Rice

September 24: I promise to go easier on drinking and go to bed earlier, but not for you fifty thousand dollars, or two hundred and fifty thousand dollars will I give up women. They're too much fun. ~ Babe Ruth

September 25: I never would say a player stinks. Ever. I'll tell you their team stinks, and first of all they know their team stinks. And the fans know their team stinks. ~ Charles Barkley

September 26: The only way I'd worry about the weather is if it snows on our side of the field and not theirs. ~ Tommy Lasorda

September 27: Reverse every natural instinct and do the opposite of what you are inclined to do, and you will

probably come very close to having the perfect golf swing.
~ Ben Hogan

September 28: I'll let the racket do the talking. ~ John McEnroe

September 29: When I was 40, my doctor advised me that a man in his 40's shouldn't play tennis. I heeded his advice carefully and could hardly wait until I reached 50 so I could start again. ~ Hugo Black

September 30: You spend a good piece of your life gripping a baseball and in the end it turns out that it was the other way around all the time. ~ Jim Bouton

October 1: What's a good tournament for him? Winning it. He's good enough. ~ Greg Norman

October 2: I'm a competitive person and I love the challenge of mastering new things. ~ Sasha Cohen

October 3: Relax? How can anybody relax and play golf? You have to grip the club don't you? ~ Ben Hogan

October 4: Gee, it's lonesome in the outfield. It's hard to keep awake with nothing to do. ~ Babe Ruth

October 5: If I weren't earning $3 million a year to dunk a basketball, most people on the street would run in the other direction. ~ Charles Barkley

October 6: If a lot of people gripped a knife and fork the way they do a golf club they would starve to death. ~ Sam Snead

October 7: I play in the low 80's. If it's any hotter than that, I won't play. ~ Joe E. Lewis

October 8: I started playing ball when I was a kid. My dad was a pro baseball player and he passed on his knowledge to me. ~ Kurt Russel

October 9: The integrity of the game is everything. ~ Peter Ueberroth

October 10: I don't know why people question the academic training of an athlete. Fifty percent of the doctors in this country graduated in the bottom half of their class. ~ Al McGuire

October 11: Baseball is drama with an endless run and an ever-changing cast. ~ Joe Garagiola

October 12: I had pro offers from the Detroit Lions, and the Green Bay Packers, who were pretty hard up for linemen in those days. If I had gone into professional football, the name Jerry Ford may have been a household word today. ~ Gerald R. Ford

October 13: Some people are born on third base and go through life thinking they hit a triple. ~ Barry Switzer

October 14: I didn't mean to hit the umpire with the dirt, but I did mean to hit that bastard in the stands. ~ Babe Ruth

October 15: It ain't like we're curing cancer or anything, we're playing basketball. ~ Charles Barkley

October 16: The only way to prove you're a good sport is to lose. ~ Ernie Banks

October 17: Baseball life is a tough life on the family. ~ Nolan Ryan

October 18: What other people may find in poetry or art museums, I find in the flight of a good drive. ~ Arnold Palmer

October 19: My family knew, but most of the sporting world did not realize that my right hand been some 75% paralyzed. ~ Bill Toomey

October 20: The only thing a golfer needs is more daylight. ~ Ben Hogan

October 21: Golf is a day spent in a round of strenuous idleness. ~ William Wordsworth

October 22: Have you ever noticed what golf spells backwards. ~ Al Boliska

October 23: Nobody's a natural. You work hard to get good and then work to get better. It's hard to stay on top. ~ Paul Coffey

October 24: I learned early to drink beer, wine, and whiskey. And I think I was about 5 when I first chewed tobacco. ~ Babe Ruth

October 25: Just because you say something doesn't make it controversial, and it doesn't make you a bad person. ~ Charles Barkley

October 26: Bulls do not win bullfights. People do. ~ Norman Ralph Augustine

October 27: Most ball games are lost not won. ~ Casey Stengel

October 28: Sometimes in football you have to score goals. ~ Thierry Henry

October 29: Tennis is a perfect combination of violent actions taking place in an atmosphere of total tranquility. ~ Billy Jean-King

October 30: You can make a lot of money in this game. Just ask my ex-wives. Both of them are so rich that neither of their husbands work. ~ Lee Trevino

November 1: Baseball is almost the only orderly thing in a very unorderly world. If you get three strikes, even the best lawyer in the world can't get you off. ~ Bill Veeck

November 2: The trouble with jogging is the ice falls out of your glass. ~ Martin Mull

November 3: All sports for all people. ~ Pierre de Coubertin

November 4: If I just tried for them dinky singles I could've batted around .600. ~ Babe Ruth

November 5: Kids are great. That's one of the best things about our business, all the kids you get to meet. It's a shame they have to grow up to be regular people and come to the games and call you names. ~ Charles Barkley

November 6: If you watch a game it's fun. If you play it, it's recreation. If you work at it, it's golf. ~ Bob Hope

November 7: There isn't a flaw in his golf or his makeup. He will win more majors than Arnold Palmer and me combined. Somebody is going to dust my records. It might as well be Tiger, because he's such a great kid. ~ Jack Nicklaus

November 8: He has the finest fundamentally sound golf swing I've ever seen. ~ Jack Nicklaus

November 9: Golf is a game in which one endeavors to control a ball with implements ill adapted for the purpose. ~ Woodrow Wilson

November 10: If you've got game, you've got game. That's why Tiger Woods is out there playing golf with Greg Norman. ~ Shaquille O'Neal

November 11: Wrestling is ballet with violence. ~ Jesse Ventura

November 12: I know I'm getting better at golf because I'm hitting fewer spectators. ~ Gerald R. Ford

November 13: Life is about timing. ~ Carl Lewis

November 14: How about a little noise? How do you expect a man to putt? ~ Babe Ruth

November 15: Look, I'm in the top 20 players who ever lived. ~ Charles Barkley

November 16: The game of golf would lose a great deal if croquet mallets and billiard cues were allowed on the putting green. ~ Ernest Hemingway

November 17: I won't predict anything historic, but nothing is impossible. ~ Micahel Phelps

November 18: Success is where preparation and opportunity meet. ~ Bobby Unser

November 19: If you drink, don't drive. Don't even putt. ~ Dean Martin

November 20: It's a round ball, a round bat, and you got to hit it square. ~ Pet Rose

November 21: I'd just as soon play tennis with the net down. ~ Robert Frost

November 22: If you meet Buddha in the lane, feed him the ball. ~ Phil Jackson

November 23: Skiing combines outdoor fun with knocking down trees with your face. ~ Dave Berry

November 24: All I can tell them is pick a good one and sock it. I get back to the dugout and they ask me what it was I hit and I tell them I don't know except it looked good. ~ Babe Ruth

November 25: The main thing to do is relax and let your talent do the work. ~ Charles Barkley

November 26: You don't play against opponents, you play against the game of basketball. ~ Bobby Knight

November 27: Fans don't boo nobodies. ~ Reggie Jackson

November 28: I regard golf as an expensive way of playing marbles. ~ Gilbert K. Chesterton

November 29: Golf is a game where you yell "fore" shoot six and write down five. ~ Paul Harvey

November 30: I guess there is nothing that will get your mind off everything like golf. I have never been depressed enough to take up the game, but they say you get so sore at yourself, you forget to hate your enemies. ~ Will Rogers

December 1: God made me fast and when I run, I feel his pleasure. ~ Eric Liddell

December 2: Give me golf clubs, fresh air, and a beautiful partner, and you can keep the clubs and the fresh air. ~ Jack Benny

December 3: A lifetime of efforts for just ten seconds. ~ Jesse Owens

December 4: If it wasn't for baseball, I'd be in either the penitentiary or the cemetery. ~ Babe Ruth

December 5: One thing about being famous is the people around you, you pay all their bills so they very rarely disagree with you because they want you to pick up the check. ~ Charles Barkley

December 6: Approach the game with no preset agendas and you'll probably be surprised at your overall efforts. ~ Phil Jackson

December 7: Baseball is a game where a curve is an optical illusion, a screwball can be a pitch or a person, stealing is legal, and you can spit anywhere you like except in the umpire's eye and on the ball. ~ James Patrick Murray

December 8: You wouldn't have won if we'd beaten you. ~ Yogi Berra

December 9: Basketball is like war in that offensive weapons are developed first, and it always takes a while for the defense to catch up. ~ Red Auerbach

December 10: You can't win unless you learn how to lose. ~ Kareem Abdul-Jabbar

December 11: You win some, lose some, and wreck some. ~ Dale Earnhardt

December 12: The only time my prayers are never answered is on the golf course. ~ Billy Graham

December 13: Fishing is much more than fish. It is a great occasion when we may return to the fine simplicity of our forefathers. ~ Herbert Hoover

December 14: I won't be happy until we have every boy in America between the ages of six and sixteen wearing a glove and swinging a bat. ~ Babe Ruth

December 15: The only difference between a good shot and a bad shot is if it goes in or not. ~ Charles Barkley

December 16: Baseball happens to be a game of cumulative tension but football, basketball, and hockey are played with hand grenades and machine guns. ~ John Leonard

December 17: Champions keep playing until they get it right. ~ Billie Jean King

December 18: Baseball has the great advantage over cricket of being over sooner. ~ George Bernard Shaw

December 19: Baseball players are smarter than football players. How often do you see a baseball team penalized for too many men on the field? ~ Jim Bouton

December 20: If you think it's hard to meet new people try picking up the wrong golf ball. ~ Jack Lemmon

December 21: Academe, n: An ancient school where morality and philosophy were taught. Academy, n: A modern school were football is taught. ~ Ambrose Bierce

December 22: Football is an incredible game. Sometimes it is so incredible it's unbelievable. ~ Tom Landry

December 23: Baseball is the only field of endeavor where a man can succeed three times out of ten and be considered a good performer. ~ Ted Williams

December 24: Paris ain't much of a town. ~Babe Ruth

December 25: What I try to do is, I just want the fans to enjoy the game. ~ Charles Barkley

December 26: All the hockey players I know are bilingual. They know English and profanity. ~ Gordie Howe

December 27: I am building a fire, and every day I train, I add more fuel. At just the right moment I light the match. ~ Mia Hamm

December 28: I see great things in baseball. It's our game—the American game. ~ Walt Whitman

December 29: Winning is a habit, unfortunately so is losing. ~ Vince Lombardi

December 30: Most people never run far enough on their first wind to find out they have a second. ~ William James

December 31: Well, all I can say is that people know I'm not saying anything out of malice. ~ Charles Barkley

Collect all the 365 Days of Happiness Books

365 Days of America
365 Days of Cats
365 Days of Dogs
365 Days of Horses
365 Days of Romance
365 Days of Sports
365 Days of the Bible